Whitfield editions

Breakout
DINOSAURS

Hugh Brewster
and the curators of the Royal Ontario Museum

Illustrated by Alan Barnard

BREAKOUT!

When we look at dinosaurs in the museum, we imagine them alive. Maybe you'd like to add flesh to their bones and see them roaring — baring their enormous teeth. Perhaps you'd even like to see them break out of their displays and charge through the building! (You know that this couldn't happen, of course, since dinosaurs died out millions of years ago.)

But maybe you don't know just how many of these amazing creatures once lived right here in Canada. If you walk in some parts of Alberta's Dinosaur Provincial Park, for example, you'll likely be stepping on dino bones and teeth. It is the single richest fossil site in the world — over 500 skeletons of 36 different kinds of dinosaurs have been uncovered there.

If you want to discover dinosaurs, Canada is one of the best countries in the world in which to look.

CANADA

WHEN THE DINOSAURS RULED

Seventy million years ago, large areas of Canada were underwater. A shallow inland seaway flowed from the Arctic down to the Caribbean. Alberta had a wide coastline along its shores where dinosaurs feasted on the lush greenery that grew in its swampy river deltas.

B.C. Dino Tracks

In 2001, nine-year-old Daniel Helm and 11-year-old Mark Turner discovered what they thought were dinosaur tracks near Tumbler Ridge, B.C. They contacted paleontologist Rich McCrea, who identified them as footprints from an armadillo-like ankylosaur. A dig nearby uncovered dino bones that were 93 million years old.

ANKYLOSAUR

WESTERN SEAWAY

HUD

Edmonton Duckbills

Bones from duck-billed dinosaurs called *hadrosaurs* have been found within the Edmonton city limits.

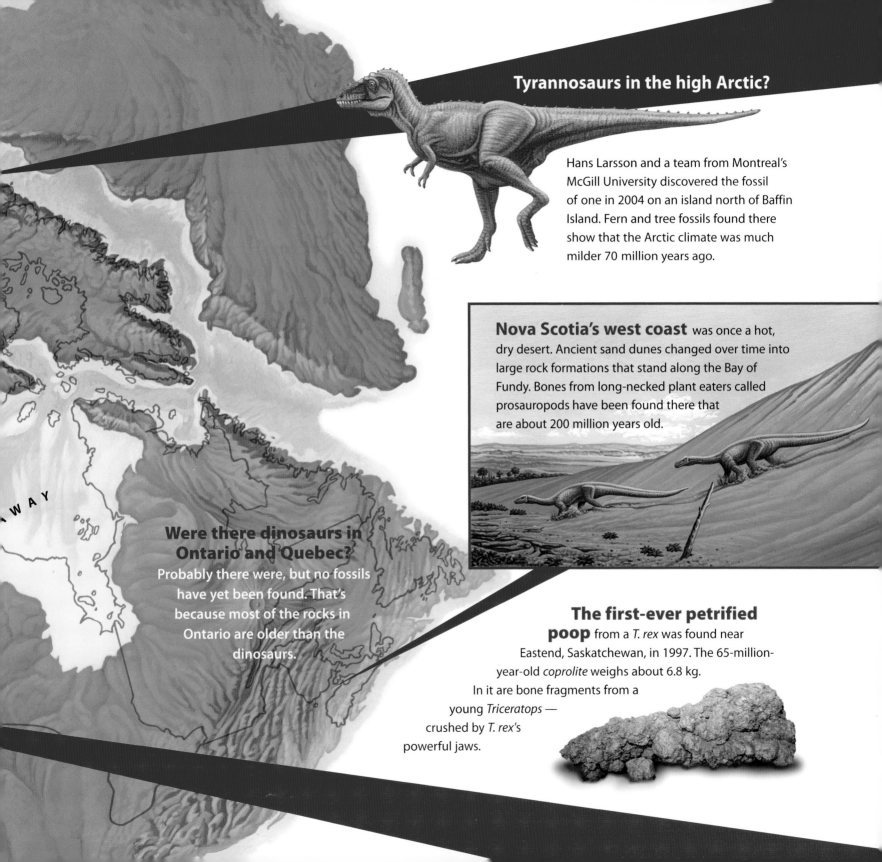

Tyrannosaurs in the high Arctic?

Hans Larsson and a team from Montreal's McGill University discovered the fossil of one in 2004 on an island north of Baffin Island. Fern and tree fossils found there show that the Arctic climate was much milder 70 million years ago.

Nova Scotia's west coast was once a hot, dry desert. Ancient sand dunes changed over time into large rock formations that stand along the Bay of Fundy. Bones from long-necked plant eaters called prosauropods have been found there that are about 200 million years old.

Were there dinosaurs in Ontario and Quebec?

Probably there were, but no fossils have yet been found. That's because most of the rocks in Ontario are older than the dinosaurs.

The first-ever petrified poop

from a *T. rex* was found near Eastend, Saskatchewan, in 1997. The 65-million-year-old *coprolite* weighs about 6.8 kg. In it are bone fragments from a young *Triceratops* — crushed by *T. rex*'s powerful jaws.

They were some of the largest, fiercest carnivores the world has ever seen. And they roamed through Alberta 85 to 65 million years ago. Everybody's favourite scary dino, *Tyrannosaurus rex*, was the king of the "tyrant lizards" — which is just what its name means. As long as a school bus and as heavy as two elephants, *T. rex* had the most powerful bite of any animal that has ever lived. Its huge teeth were serrated like steak knives and could chomp right through flesh and bones.

BIG AND DEADLY

ALBERTA'S TYRANNOSAURS

Another Alberta tyrannosaur — named *Albertosaurus* — was smaller than *T. rex*, but was every bit as vicious. With its long legs it may have been the fastest of all the tyrannosaurs — able to chase down the duck-billed dinos on which it feasted.

If a *T. rex* fought an *Albertosaurus*, who would win?
Neither, because *Albertosaurus* died out a million years before *T. rex* came on the scene.

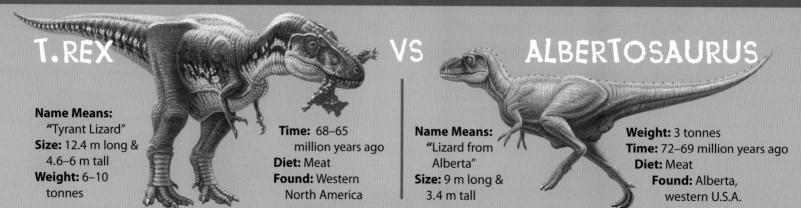

T. REX VS ALBERTOSAURUS

Name Means:
"Tyrant Lizard"
Size: 12.4 m long & 4.6–6 m tall
Weight: 6–10 tonnes

Time: 68–65 million years ago
Diet: Meat
Found: Western North America

Name Means:
"Lizard from Alberta"
Size: 9 m long & 3.4 m tall

Weight: 3 tonnes
Time: 72–69 million years ago
Diet: Meat
Found: Alberta, western U.S.A.

An Albertosaurus uses its powerful jaws to bring down a duck-billed Hypacrosaurus.

SEA MONSTERS OVER

Canada's shallow inland sea swarmed with strange marine reptiles (which were not dinosaurs). The long-necked elasmosaur gobbled fish with its powerful jaws and teeth. It could be up to 14 metres long, and over half of that length was neck. A mosasaur could be a metre longer and looked like a giant crocodile with flippers. It could snag large fish or even small sharks with its massive teeth.

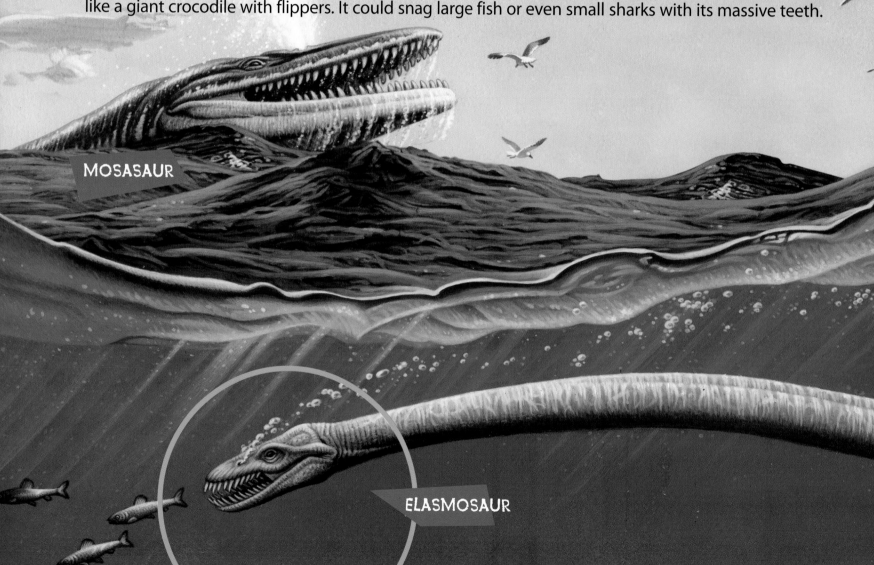

MOSASAUR

ELASMOSAUR

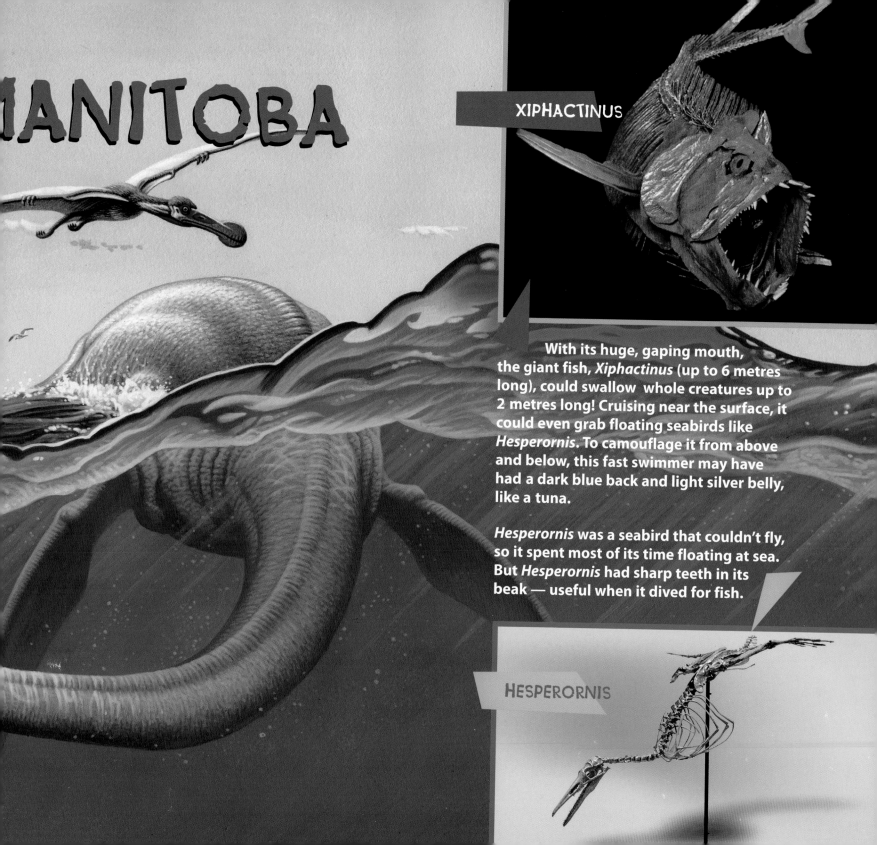

MANITOBA

XIPHACTINUS

With its huge, gaping mouth, the giant fish, *Xiphactinus* (up to 6 metres long), could swallow whole creatures up to 2 metres long! Cruising near the surface, it could even grab floating seabirds like *Hesperornis*. To camouflage it from above and below, this fast swimmer may have had a dark blue back and light silver belly, like a tuna.

Hesperornis was a seabird that couldn't fly, so it spent most of its time floating at sea. But *Hesperornis* had sharp teeth in its beak — useful when it dived for fish.

HESPERORNIS

150 MILLION YEARS AGO

A WESTERN SHOWDOWN

Screams and roars pierced the dusty air as the *Stegosaurus* swung its heavy tail. The *Allosaurus* howled as the metre-long spikes from the stegosaur's tail sank into its neck. Two other allosaurs from the pack came to help. They circled around the stegosaur, whose tail spikes had become firmly stuck in the first allosaur's back. One allosaur ripped the stegosaur's belly with its sharp claws while the other tried to bite its head. The stegosaur was no match for the huge predators and soon toppled, bleeding, on its side. Before long, the three allosaurs gorged greedily on their prey.

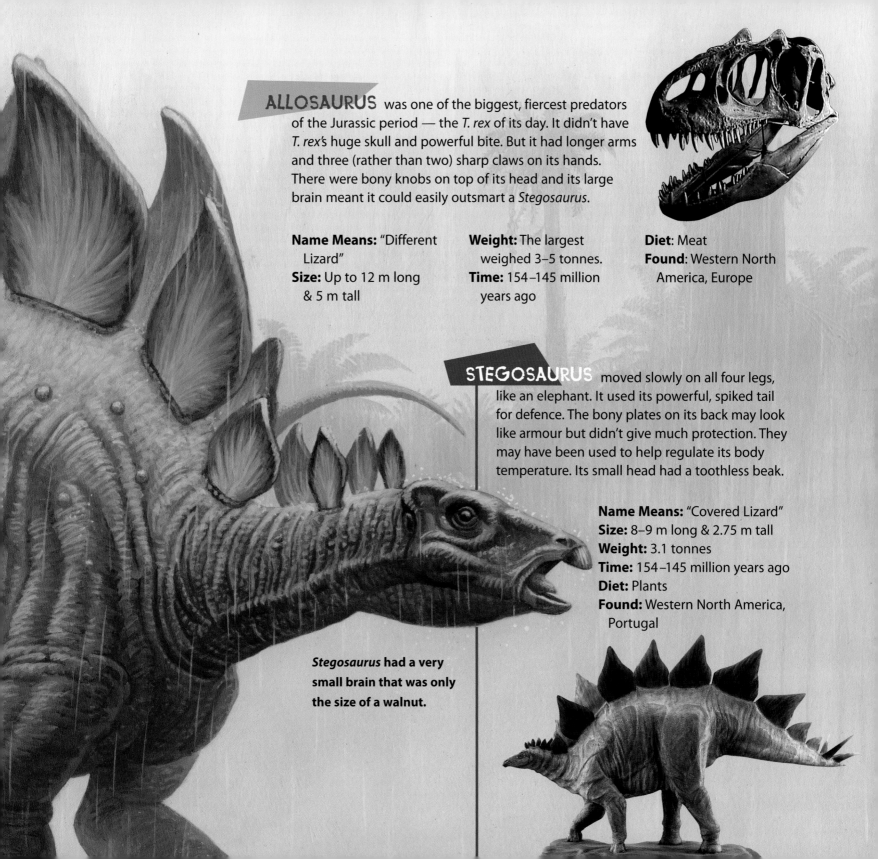

ALLOSAURUS was one of the biggest, fiercest predators of the Jurassic period — the *T. rex* of its day. It didn't have *T. rex*'s huge skull and powerful bite. But it had longer arms and three (rather than two) sharp claws on its hands. There were bony knobs on top of its head and its large brain meant it could easily outsmart a *Stegosaurus*.

Name Means: "Different Lizard"
Size: Up to 12 m long & 5 m tall

Weight: The largest weighed 3–5 tonnes.
Time: 154–145 million years ago

Diet: Meat
Found: Western North America, Europe

STEGOSAURUS moved slowly on all four legs, like an elephant. It used its powerful, spiked tail for defence. The bony plates on its back may look like armour but didn't give much protection. They may have been used to help regulate its body temperature. Its small head had a toothless beak.

Name Means: "Covered Lizard"
Size: 8–9 m long & 2.75 m tall
Weight: 3.1 tonnes
Time: 154–145 million years ago
Diet: Plants
Found: Western North America, Portugal

Stegosaurus had a very small brain that was only the size of a walnut.

JURASSIC GIANTS

They were the largest animals that have ever lived on land. With their long necks, sauropods could reach plants and leaves which they gobbled down whole. *Brachiosaurus* (opposite) held its neck upright like a giraffe's so it could reach high trees. *Diplodocus* (below) stood with its neck straight out so that it could poke into forests to scoop up ferns, leaves, and soft plants.

Down East Ancestors

Canada's oldest dinosaurs are the prosauropods found on Nova Scotia's west coast (see page 5). Fifty million years later, these elephant-sized plant eaters would evolve into giant sauropods that were ten times larger.

DIPLODOCUS

was longer than two school buses and had a whip-like tail that it could crack like a bullwhip. It walked on four legs the size of tree trunks, and each foot had a sharp thumb claw that may have been used for fighting. *Diplodocus* babies were hatched from eggs and may have lived for as long as 50 years.

Name Means: "Double Beamed" because its spine had double-pronged bones that may have helped keep its long tail off the ground.
Size: 27 m long with an 8 m neck and 14 m tail
Weight: 9–18 tonnes
Time: 154–144 million years ago
Diet: Plants
Found: Western North America

Our first Sauropods Until 2002, no sauropods had been found in Canada. That year, dinosaur footprint expert Rich McCrea found a sauropod trackway in British Columbia. Now we know that these giants made the earth in Canada tremble 150 million years ago.

BRACHIOSAURUS needed a very powerful heart to pump blood up its long neck to its brain (even though it had a relatively small brain like most sauropods). Scientists think a brachiosaur's blood pressure must have been three or four times as high as ours. Unlike *Diplodocus*, a brachiosaur had a short, thick tail and front legs that were longer than its hind legs.

Name Means: "Arm Lizard"
Size: 26 m long &
   12–16 m tall
Weight: 30–80 tonnes
Time: 154–144 million
   years ago
Diet: Plants
Found: Western North
   America, Africa

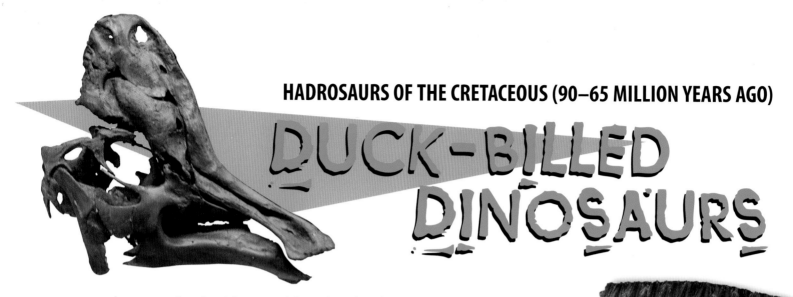

DUCK-BILLED DINOSAURS

Hadrosaurs had wide, toothless beaks that looked like a duck's bill. Their beaks were good for nipping off plants that were then chewed by an amazing set of teeth. You probably have around 32 teeth. A hadrosaur had as many as 200 — with three to five replacements stacked underneath each one!

There were two main kinds of hadrosaurs. Some had flat skulls and were plainer looking, while others had strange head crests like the one on *Corythosaurus,* seen opposite. These hollow crests came in many different shapes and were probably used to create noises that could attract mates or warn others of danger. Their ability to live together and protect each other was likely an important factor in the success of the hadrosaurs.

Towards the end of the Cretaceous period, as the number of dinosaurs declined, hadrosaurs were among the survivors.

This piece of a hadrosaur's jaw shows its many teeth. As each tooth wore down, a new one was right there to replace it.

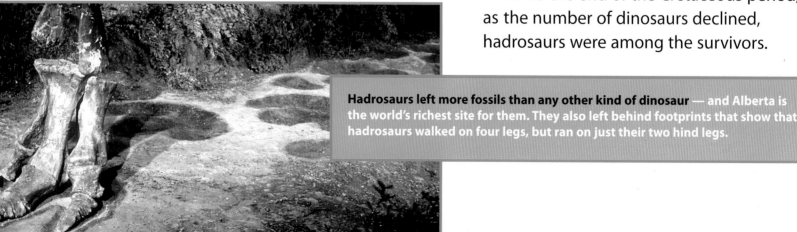

Hadrosaurs left more fossils than any other kind of dinosaur — and Alberta is the world's richest site for them. They also left behind footprints that show that hadrosaurs walked on four legs, but ran on just their two hind legs.

Some corythosaurs ("helmet lizards") pass through an ancient forest. They were about 9–10 metres long and weighed up to 4.5 tonnes.

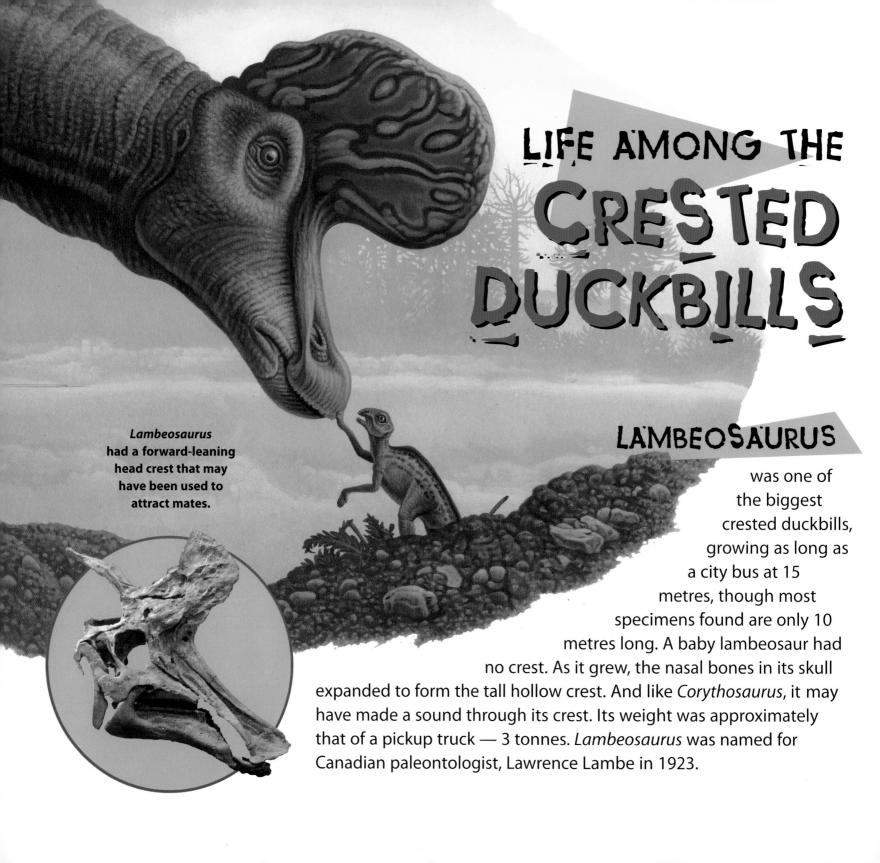

LIFE AMONG THE CRESTED DUCKBILLS

Lambeosaurus had a forward-leaning head crest that may have been used to attract mates.

LAMBEOSAURUS

was one of the biggest crested duckbills, growing as long as a city bus at 15 metres, though most specimens found are only 10 metres long. A baby lambeosaur had no crest. As it grew, the nasal bones in its skull expanded to form the tall hollow crest. And like *Corythosaurus*, it may have made a sound through its crest. Its weight was approximately that of a pickup truck — 3 tonnes. *Lambeosaurus* was named for Canadian paleontologist, Lawrence Lambe in 1923.

PARASAUROLOPHUS had perhaps the most spectacular crest of all the hadrosaurs. It was hollow and bony and could be up to 1.8 metres long. And there was a notch where the end of the crest touched the creature's back. The crest had four tubes inside it that may have been used to produce a low sound like a foghorn. Scientists believe that each species of *Parasaurolophus* may have made a distinctive sound that others could recognize. Fossils show us that it had a pebbly-textured hide and it is often depicted with coloured skin. We don't know exactly what colour dinosaurs were, but we assume that some of them had beautiful colours like modern lizards. From its beak to its pointed tail, *Parasaurolophus* was 10–12 metres long, and at 3,500 kilograms weighed as much as an elephant.

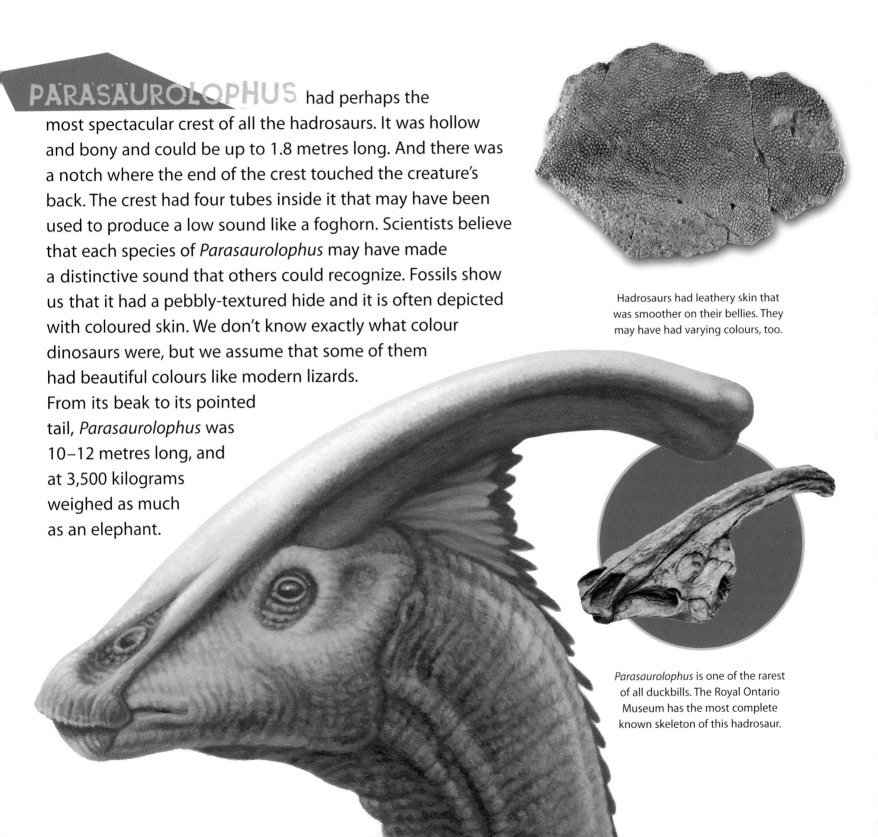

Hadrosaurs had leathery skin that was smoother on their bellies. They may have had varying colours, too.

Parasaurolophus is one of the rarest of all duckbills. The Royal Ontario Museum has the most complete known skeleton of this hadrosaur.

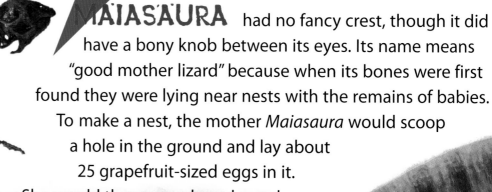

MAIASAURA had no fancy crest, though it did have a bony knob between its eyes. Its name means "good mother lizard" because when its bones were first found they were lying near nests with the remains of babies. To make a nest, the mother *Maiasaura* would scoop a hole in the ground and lay about 25 grapefruit-sized eggs in it. She would then spread sand over her eggs and cover them with leaves and plants. As the plants rotted, they would keep the eggs warm. The newly-hatched babies were about 30 centimetres in length (above), but an adult *Maiasaura* would grow to be roughly nine metres long. It likely lived in large herds and migrated with the seasons.

FLAT-SKULLED HADROSAURS

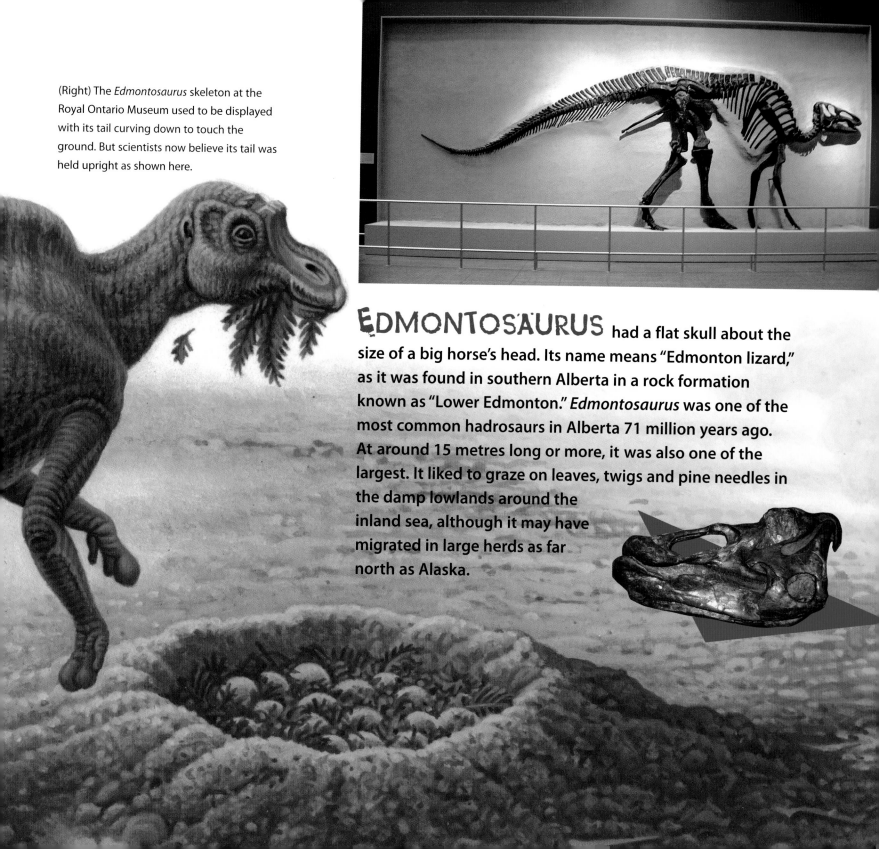

(Right) The *Edmontosaurus* skeleton at the Royal Ontario Museum used to be displayed with its tail curving down to touch the ground. But scientists now believe its tail was held upright as shown here.

EDMONTOSAURUS had a flat skull about the size of a big horse's head. Its name means "Edmonton lizard," as it was found in southern Alberta in a rock formation known as "Lower Edmonton." *Edmontosaurus* was one of the most common hadrosaurs in Alberta 71 million years ago. At around 15 metres long or more, it was also one of the largest. It liked to graze on leaves, twigs and pine needles in the damp lowlands around the inland sea, although it may have migrated in large herds as far north as Alaska.

HERDS OF HORNS

Huge herds of horned and frilled dinosaurs once lumbered across North America. *Triceratops* is one of the most famous of them. But 14 different kinds of horned dinos (called ceratopsians) have been found in Alberta. All were four-footed plant eaters and had bulky bodies, short tails and parrot-like beaks. Each species had a different-shaped frill topped by horns and spikes. The frills of most horned dinosaurs were too thin to have given much protection from an attack by a predator such as *T. rex*. But the horns on the elephant-sized *Triceratops* were known to have caused damage when used in a fight.

CHASMOSAURUS had the showiest frill of all, with large holes or "chasms" in it. Scientists now believe these frills were mainly used for display during mating season — like a wild turkey fanning its tail in spring. So its frill may well have been brightly coloured as shown here. Dinosaurs probably had eyes that could see in colour, like birds do today.

CENTROSAURUS means "sharp point lizard," which describes its many horns. Its main, curved horn was 46 cm. long and its bony frill had small spikes around the edges. We know the centrosaurs lived in herds because of the many bone beds found in Alberta. Three bone beds in Dinosaur Provincial Park contain the remains of 300 to 1000 animals each.

What would cause all these huge animals to be found dead together? Scientists believe that whole herds of centrosaurs may have drowned in flooding caused by violent typhoons or hurricanes.

WALKING TANKS

EDMONTONIA was a little smaller than *Euoplocephalus* and had short legs and no tail club. Four large spikes jutted down from its shoulders. These may have been used in contests of strength with other ankylosaurs. For protection, it probably crouched down to guard its underbelly. *Edmontonia* had a long, flat skull with small teeth and weak jaws, which limited its diet to soft plants like ferns. Very few fossils of this dinosaur have been found — maybe because there just weren't that many of them. Its name means "from Edmonton," as it was found in rocks known as the "Edmonton Formation" in southern Alberta.

They waddled along looking like armoured tanks. Bony armour and studs and spikes gave them protection — some of them even had armoured eyelids! *Euoplocephalus*, seen below, was the largest of the four ankylosaurs found in Alberta. It was about the size of a minivan. Only when flipped over could it be wounded.

EUOPLOCEPHALUS

Name Means: "True plated head"
Size: 6–7 m long
Weight: 1.8 tonnes
Time: 76.5–69 million years ago

Diet: Low lying-plants
Found: Western North America

Euoplocephalus's

bony tail club could weigh up to 30 kilograms. It was a mean wrecking ball and would likely have broken the leg of any attacking tyrannosaur.

PHEW!

Did an Ankylosaur Pass Here?

Ankylosaurs had to eat many low-lying plants with tough stems which likely fermented in their large guts — producing lots of

SMELLY GAS!

Did birds evolve from dinosaurs? Most scientists think they did. Birds first appeared about 150 million years ago. Their ancestors were small dinosaurs that had three-toed feet, hollow bones, and sat on nests — just like birds. They were relatives of the dromaeosaurs, a group of dinosaurs that later included *Velociraptor* (above) and *Utahraptor* (opposite). Although they weren't birds, these two dinosaurs also had feathers and claws.

FEATHERS & CLAWS

The First Feathered Dinosaur

In 1996, Canadian scientist Philip Currie helped identify the first feathered dinosaur fossil ever found (below). It was named *Sinosauropteryx* ("Chinese lizard wing"), since it was found in China. This tiny dinosaur lived from 135–121 million years ago and had downy fuzz along its back and sides. In this very fine, furry covering, scientists can detect the beginnings of feathers.

Smaller dinosaurs like this one probably lived in Canada, too, although their bones have not been found here yet.

Sinosauropteryx was about 1.25 metres long and ate small animals and insects.

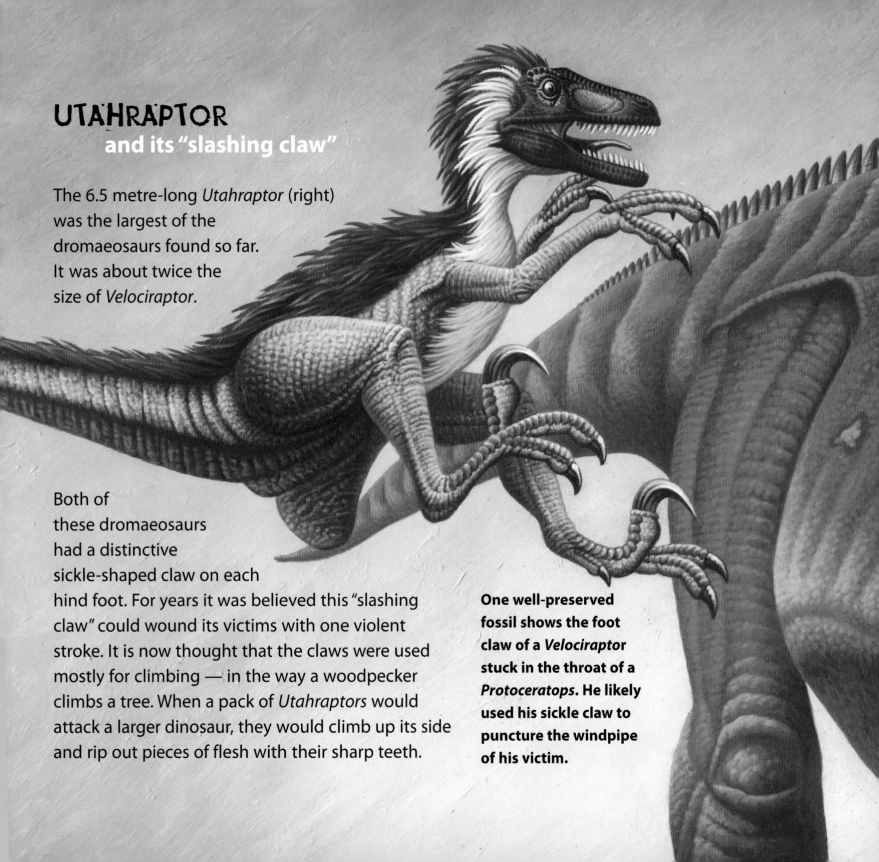

UTAHRAPTOR
and its "slashing claw"

The 6.5 metre-long *Utahraptor* (right) was the largest of the dromaeosaurs found so far. It was about twice the size of *Velociraptor*.

Both of these dromaeosaurs had a distinctive sickle-shaped claw on each hind foot. For years it was believed this "slashing claw" could wound its victims with one violent stroke. It is now thought that the claws were used mostly for climbing — in the way a woodpecker climbs a tree. When a pack of *Utahraptors* would attack a larger dinosaur, they would climb up its side and rip out pieces of flesh with their sharp teeth.

One well-preserved fossil shows the foot claw of a *Velociraptor* stuck in the throat of a *Protoceratops*. He likely used his sickle claw to puncture the windpipe of his victim.

FEATHERED OVIRAPTORS

When the first *Oviraptor* was discovered in the Gobi Desert in 1924, it was sitting on top of some eggs. So the scientists gave it a name that means "egg robber." Later discoveries showed that the *Oviraptor* was actually *guarding* the eggs, not eating them. But it probably *did* eat other dinosaurs' eggs, as well as meat, seeds, insects and plants.

OVIRAPTOR

was a small dinosaur (1.8–2.5 m long) that could move fast on its two hind legs. For years it was depicted as having a lizard-like skin, but it is now believed to have had feathers, as shown opposite. It also had a toothless beak and a skull like a bird's. Very few oviraptors have been found in Canada. One, called *Caenagnathus*, chased small reptiles and mammals along Alberta's seashore 74 million years ago.

(Opposite) An Oviraptor *spreads its big-clawed fingers and lashes out with feathered arms as two* Velociraptors *circle in for an attack. (Left) A fossilized* Oviraptor *nest shows what the eggs it was protecting looked like.*

A Buck-Toothed Relative

It was about the size of a turkey and lived in China 120 million years ago. It is also the oldest known oviraptor — and one of the world's weirdest dinos. *Incisivosaurus* ("incisor lizard") is named for its large, beaver-like front teeth. Some people have dubbed it "the rabbitosaurus," since, like a rabbit, it was a gnawer, chewing away on tree bark and pine cones.

With an eerie, brilliant light, it lit up the sky. The flaming asteroid then slammed into the earth, blasting enormous chunks of rock into the air. Earthquakes, dust clouds and acid rain followed, wiping out more than half of all the plants and animals on earth — including the dinosaurs.

But is the "killer asteroid" the *only* reason the dinosaurs became extinct? Most scientists think it was just "the last straw."

65 MILLION YEARS AGO

WIPEOUT!

By the time the asteroid crashed into Mexico, the shallow seas that once covered the Prairies had dried up. The lush deltas where the hadrosaurs had nibbled on flowering plants were gone. The climate had become cooler, and many dinosaurs may not have survived the colder winters.

To make matters worse, huge volcanoes had exploded in different parts of the world during these years. Plants and animals would have suffered from the massive clouds of ash and poisonous gas. So, when the asteroid struck, the dinosaurs that were left were finished off. Perhaps if it had landed in an earlier time, some of them might have survived.

But the dinosaurs that evolved into birds *did* survive. From small, ancient dinosaurs came the 9,300 kinds of birds that we know today. And when you look at an ostrich or the claws of a woodpecker, you can see that dinosaurs are not only found in museum displays. They are with us still.

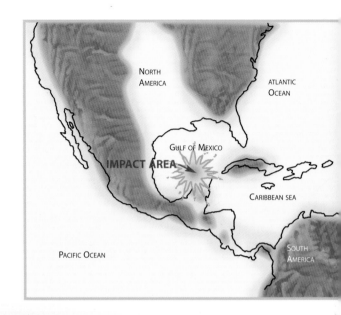

The asteroid hit near the Yucatan peninsula of Mexico. Craters from the explosion have been found thousands of miles away. (Below) A Triceratops *dies in a forest fire caused by the flaming asteroid.*

When the Dinosaurs Ruled

TRIASSIC:
250-200 million years ago

JURASSIC:
200-145 million years ago

CRETACEOUS:
145-65 million years ago

TODAY

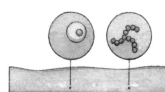

First single cell
3.5 billion
years ago

Blue-green
algae

Wormlike organisms
with spinal cords

Jawless fish

Land plants

Amphibians

Reptiles

PALEOZOIC ERA
540–250 million years ago

Glossary

asteroid: a celestial body that is smaller than a planet but larger than a meteorite and that usually orbits around the sun

coprolite: fossilized excrement

dinosaurs: Land-dwelling animals that lived on Earth from 225 to 65 million years ago. Their legs were right under their bodies and did not stick out from their sides like a lizard's. Not all ancient creatures were dinosaurs, especially those that swam or flew.

Mesozoic: The scientific name for the era during which the dinosaurs lived. It is divided into three periods: the **Triassic** (250-200 million years ago), the **Jurassic** (200–145 million years ago) and the **Cretaceous** (145–65 million years ago).

paleontologist: a scientist who studies life in prehistoric times

sickle: a tool with a curved blade and short handle used for cutting grass or wheat

Pronunciation Guide

Allosaurus: **AL oh SORE us**
ankylosaur: **an KIE loh SORE**
Albertosaurus: **al BERT oh SORE us**
Brachiosaurus: **brake e oh SORE us**
Caenagnathus: **SEE nag NAY thus**
ceratopsians: **SER uh TOP see ins**
Centrosaurus: **SEN tro SORE us**
Chasmosaurus: **KAZ moh SORE us**
Corythosaurus: **koh RITH oh SORE us**
Diplodocus: **dip PLOD oh kuss**
dromaeosaurs: **DROH mee oh SORES**
Edmontonia: **ED mon TOH nee uh**
Edmontosaurus: **ed MON toh SORE us**
elasmosaur: **eh LAZZ mo SORE**
Euoplocephalus: **YOO oh ploh SEF uh lus**
hadrosaur: **HAD roh SORE**
Hesperornis: **Hes per ORN is**

Hypacrosaurus: **hye PACK ro SORE us**
Incisivosaurus: **in siz ee voh SORE us**
Lambeosaurus: **LAM bee oh SORE us**
Maiasaura: **my ah SORE ah**
mosasaur: **MOZ ah SORE**
Oviraptor: **OH vih RAP tore**
Parasaurolophus: **PAR ah sore AWL loff us**
prosauropods: **pro SORE oh pods**
Protoceratops: **proto SER uh TOPS**
sauropods: **SORE oh pods**
Sinosauropteryx: **SIEN oh sore OP ter iks**
Stegosaurus: **steg OSS er us**
Triceratops: **trye SAIR a tops**
Tyrannosaurus: **tye RAN oh SORE us**
Utahraptor: **YOO tah RAP tore**
Velociraptor: **vel OSS ih RAP tore**
Xiphactinus: **zie FAK tin us**

The first dinosaurs lived approximately 220 million years ago, during the Triassic period. The last of them were gone by the end of the Cretaceous period, 65 million years ago. The early dinosaurs lived on a single land mass called Pangaea. During the Jurassic and Cretaceous periods, Earth's continents drifted farther and farther apart until the globe finally resembled the world we know today.

y dinosaurs   Mammals   *Allosaurus*   *Stegosaurus*   *Triceratops*   *Tyrannosaurus rex*   *Modern humans*
200,000 years ago

MESOZOIC ERA
250–65 million years ago

Recommended Reading

Canadian Dinosaurs
by Erin Kelsey. A Wow Canada book.
Maple Tree Press.
A dinosaur tour from coast to coast.

Daniel's Dinosaurs
by Charles Helm. Maple Tree Press.
*The true story of two boys who
discovered dinosaur tracks in B.C.*

Digging Canadian Dinosaurs
by Rebecca Grambo and Dianna
Bonder. Walrus Books.
*More information about Canadian
dinosaurs and their discoverers.*

Selected Bibliography

Reid, Monty. *The Last Great Dinosaurs*. Red Deer: Red Deer College Press, 1990

Royal Tyrrell Museum. *Reading the Rocks: A Biography of Ancient Alberta*. Calgary: Red Deer Press, 2003

Spalding, David. *Into the Dinosaurs' Graveyard: Canadian Digs and Discoveries*. Toronto: Doubleday Canada, 1999

Grady, Wayne. *The Dinosaur Project*. Toronto: Macfarlane, Walter & Ross, 1993.

Currie, Philip J., Felber, Eric P. and Sovak, Jan. *A Moment in Time With Albertosaurus*. Calgary: Troodon Productions, 1998
_____. *A Moment in Time with Centrosaurus*. Calgary: Troodon Productions, 1998

Funston, Sylvia. *The Dinosaur Question and Answer Book*. Toronto: Greey de Pencier, 1992

Credits and Acknowledgements

All illustrations are by Alan Barnard and all fossils and skeletons are from the collection of the Royal Ontario Museum with the exceptions of: (p.5) *T. rex* coprolite, Royal Saskatchewan Museum; (p.9) *Xiphactinus*, Triebold Paleontology Inc.; (p.11) Stegosaur model by Stephen Czerkas, copyright 1986; (p.12) Prosauropod skeleton, Fundy Geological Museum, Parrsboro, Nova Scotia, reconstruction by DINOLAB, Salt Lake City, Utah. The visualization of the ROM on the front cover is by Finest Images, Berlin, and the diagrams on pp.30–31 are by Jack McMaster. We would like to especially acknowledge the contribution of Janet Waddington of the ROM for shepherding this project so carefully, and also the assistance of Brian Porter, Glen Ellis, Michelle Osborne and Brian Sullivan.

About the Authors

Hugh Brewster is the author of a number of award-winning books for young readers, including *Anastasia's Album, The Other Mozart, On Juno Beach, At Vimy Ridge* and *Carnation, Lily, Lily Rose*. **Alan Barnard** has illustrated many children's books including *Graveyards of the Dinosaurs* and *New Dinos*. The curators at the Royal Ontario Museum who so generously shared their time, expertise and collections in creating this book are **Janet Waddington, Kevin Seymour** and **David Evans**.

Where to see Dinosaurs in Canada

Royal Ontario Museum, Toronto
Dinosaur skeletons were first displayed in Toronto's Royal Ontario Museum in 1920 under the supervision of museum director and dinosaur discoverer William Arthur Parks. Today, in the spectacular new Michael Lee-Chin Crystal, over 350 specimens are on display in the Jim and Louise Temerty Galleries of the Age of Dinosaurs. These include 40 dinosaur specimens, with 18 complete or nearly complete skeletons and hundreds of fossils of reptiles, plants and insects that shared the land with the dinosaurs. An expanded marine section displays fossils of marine reptiles such as ichthyosaurs, as well as fish and other swimming creatures. http://www.rom.on.ca/exhibitions/nhistory/dinosaurs.php

Canadian Museum of Nature, Ottawa The Talisman Energy Fossil Gallery presents the events that led to the extinction of dinosaurs and rise of mammals roughly 85 to 35 million years ago. http://nature.ca/exhibits/exf/index_e.cfm

Dinosaur Provincial Park, Patricia, Alberta A UNESCO World Heritage Site two hours east of Calgary in the Alberta badlands, the park has an information centre and offers hikes and tours to fossil sites. http://tprc.alberta.ca/parks/dinosaur/flashindex.asp

Fundy Geological Museum, Parrsboro, Nova Scotia Some of Canada's oldest dinosaur bones are on display here. http://museum.gov.ns.ca/fgm/index.html

Royal Saskatchewan Museum, Regina See the swimming creatures that once lived in the seas over Saskatchewan in the Earth Sciences Gallery. http://www.royalsaskmuseum.ca

Royal Tyrrell Museum, Drumheller, Alberta Known as one of the world's great dinosaur museums, the Tyrrell offers hundreds of dinosaur fossils and displays along with guided tours of the badlands, a hands-on science hall, simulated fossil digs and many other programs. www.tyrrellmuseum.com

T.rex Discovery Centre, Eastend, Saskatchewan Watch paleontologists at work and see the bones of "Scotty" the *T. rex*, discovered near here in 1994. http://www.dinocountry.com/t-rex_center.html

Published in cooperation with the Royal Ontario Museum with the generous support of the Louise Hawley Stone Charitable Trust.

Illustrations copyright © 2007 Alan Barnard
Text copyright © Hugh Brewster
Design and compilation © Whitfield Editions

**Library and Archives Canada
Cataloguing in Publication**

Brewster, Hugh
Breakout dinosaurs : Canada's coolest and scariest ancient creatures return! / text by Hugh Brewster ; illustrated by Alan Barnard.
Includes bibliographical references.
ISBN 978-0-9781805-0-8

1. Dinosaurs—Canada—Juvenile literature.
I. Barnard, Alan II. Title.

QE861.5.B77 2007   j567.90971   C2007-902540-4

10 9 8 7 6 5 4 3 2 1

Art Director: Gord Sibley
Editorial Assistance: Lloyd Davis
Printing and Binding: Tien Wah Press, Singapore

Printed in Singapore

Whitfield editions
104 South Drive, Toronto, Ontario
Canada M4W 1R6